D1606924

Coyotes

by Ruth Strother

Consultant:
Blaire Van Valkenburgh
Professor
UCLA Department of Ecology and Evolutionary Biology

BEARPORT PUBLISHING

New York, New York

Credits

Cover and Title Page, © Design Pics Inc./Alamy; 4–5, © Critterbiz/Shutterstock; 6–7, © Tom Brakefield/Thinkstock; 8–9, © Kane513/Shutterstock; 10–11, © Terje Langeland/Shutterstock; 12, © National Parks Service; 12–13, © Stock Connection/SuperStock; 14, © iStockphoto/Thinkstock; 14–15, © Doug Lindstrand/Alaska Stock-Design Pics/SuperStock; 16–17, © Keith Szafranski/iStockphoto; 18, © iStockphoto/Thinkstock; 18–19, © Flirt/SuperStock; 20–21, © Tom Brakefield/Thinkstock; 22T, © Keith Szafranski/iStockphoto; 22C, © Stock Connection/SuperStock; 22B, © iStockphoto/Thinkstock; 23T, © Tom Brakefield/Thinkstock; 23B, © Kane513/Shutterstock.

Publisher: Kenn Goin
Senior Editor: Joyce Tavolacci
Creative Director: Spencer Brinker
Design: Emily Love
Photo Researcher: Arnold Ringstad

Library of Congress Cataloging-in-Publication Data

Strother, Ruth.
 Coyotes / by Ruth Strother ; consultant: Blaire Van Valkenburgh.
   p. cm. — (Wild canine pups)
  Includes bibliographical references and index.
  ISBN 978-1-61772-928-7 (library binding) — ISBN 1-61772-928-0 (library binding)
 1. Coyote—Juvenile literature. 2. Coyote—Life cycles—Juvenile literature. I. Van Valkenburgh, Blaire. II. Title.
  QL737.C22S785 2014
  599.77'25—dc23

2013004890

For more information, write to Bearport Publishing Company, Inc., 45 West 21st Street, Suite 3B, New York, New York 10010. Printed in the United States of America.

10 9 8 7 6 5 4 3 2 1

❖ Contents ❖

Meet coyote pups 4

What is a coyote? 6

The coyote family 8

Where do coyotes live? 10

Newborn pups 12

Feeding time 14

Howling pups 16

Leaving the den 18

All grown up 20

Glossary 22

Index 24

Read more 24

Learn more online 24

About the author 24

Meet coyote pups

Three coyote pups play in a hollow log near their **den**.

They are watching a bug as it crawls in the green grass.

The pups are going to **pounce** on it!

Catching bugs helps them learn to hunt.

coyote pups

What is a coyote?

Coyotes are a type of wild dog, like foxes and wolves.

In fact, coyotes look like wolves only they are much smaller.

Like other wild dogs, coyotes are great hunters.

Adult coyote size

Their large pointed ears help them find **prey**.

Their long bushy tails help them keep their balance as they run after animals.

pointed ears

bushy tail

The coyote family

Some coyotes live alone or in pairs.

Others live in small family groups
called packs.

Each pack has a male and
a female leader.

coyote pups

The other members of the pack are the leaders' pups.

Working together in a pack helps the coyotes hunt large animals, such as deer.

coyote mother

Where do coyotes live?

Coyotes live in North America and Central America.

They live in deserts, forests, and mountain areas.

Sometimes, they make their homes near people in towns and cities.

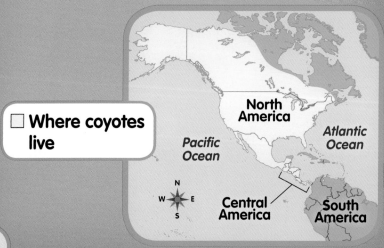

☐ **Where coyotes live**

North America

Atlantic Ocean

Pacific Ocean

N
W   E
S

Central America

South America

No matter where they live, coyotes have their own **territories**.

These are the areas where they hunt, sleep, and raise pups.

coyote
in desert

Newborn pups

A mother coyote has her babies in a hidden den.

She gives birth to about six pups.

The tiny pups are born with their eyes closed.

They also have ears that flop down.

After two weeks, their eyes open and their ears stick up straight.

young pup

coyote pups
in den

Feeding time

At first, coyote pups drink milk from their mother's body.

When they are a few weeks old, they start eating meat.

mother

coyote pup drinking milk

The pups' parents bring them rabbits, mice, and squirrels.

parent carrying rabbit

Howling pups

Young pups make sounds such as yips, howls, and barks.

They do this to **communicate** with other coyotes.

Coyotes howl to tell pack members where they are.

They bark to tell coyotes from other packs to stay away!

pup howling

17

Leaving the den

Pups explore outside the den when they are about three weeks old.

They pounce on bugs and play.

pup exploring outside the den

Playing helps them grow bigger and stronger.

After two months, the pups are ready to leave the den for good.

All grown up

When the pups are six months old,
they start hunting for their own food.

They use the skills they learned
as young pups.

When they are one year old, the coyotes are fully grown.

They are now ready to howl and hunt as adults!

young coyote chasing raccoon

Glossary

communicate
(kuh-MYOO-nuh-kayt)
to pass on information

den (DEN) a home where wild animals can rest, hide from enemies, and have babies

pounce (POUNSS)
to jump onto
something suddenly

prey (PRAY) animals that are hunted and eaten by other animals

territories (TER-uh-*tor*-eez) areas of land where animals live and hunt

Index

Central America 10

den 4, 12–13, 18–19

ears 7, 12

food 14–15, 20

habitat 10–11

hunting 4, 6–7, 9, 11, 15, 20–21

milk 14

mother 9, 12, 14

North America 10

packs 8–9, 16

playing 4–5, 18–19

prey 7, 9, 15

size 6

sounds 16

tails 7

territories 11

wolves 6

Read more

Green, Emily K. *Coyotes (Backyard Wildlife)*. Minneapolis, MN: Bellwether Media (2011).

Lunis, Natalie. *Coyote: The Barking Dog (Animal Loudmouths)*. New York: Bearport (2012).

Roza, Greg. *Your Neighbor the Coyote (City Critters)*. New York: Windmill Books (2012).

Learn more online

To learn more about coyotes, visit
www.bearportpublishing.com/WildCaninePups

About the author

Ruth Strother has written and edited numerous award-winning
books for children and adults. She has spanned the United States,
starting life in New York, growing up in Minnesota, and now living in
Southern California with her husband, daughter, and black Lab.
Her yard is frequently visited by coyotes and foxes.

DATE DUE

			PRINTED IN U.S.A.